# COMMERCIAL BEDDING PLANT PRODUCTION

Andrew Eames

Grower Guide No. 1
2nd Series

**Grower Books**
Nexus Business Communications, Kent

Grower Books
Nexus Business Communications Ltd
Warwick House
Swanley, Kent  BR8 8HY

First published 1994

© Grower Books 1994

ISBN 1 899372 00 8

Series editor Peter Rogers.          Production Christina Bunce.
Publisher Tony Salter.                Cover design Yvette Woolett.

Printed in Great Britain.

All rights reserved. This book is protected by copyright; no part of it may be reproduced, stored in a retrieval system or transmitted in any form or by any means electronic, mechanical, photocopying, recording or otherwise, without written permission from the publishers.

# Contents

| | | |
|---|---|---|
| Introduction | | 2 |

**PART 1 Production planning**

| | | |
|---|---|---|
| 1. | Basic considerations | 3 |
| | What is a bedding plant? Ways of marketing. | |
| | Seeds, seedlings or plugs. Production facilities. | |
| 2. | Boxes, packs or pots? | 8 |
| 3. | What to grow | 10 |
| | The bedding plant year. Standard bedding plants, ageratum to zinnia. | |
| 4. | The growing medium | 24 |
| | Types of compost. Peat philosophy. | |
| 5. | Feeding & fertilisers | 26 |
| | Three types of plant nutrition. Proprietary composts. | |

**PART 2 Growing the crop**

| | | |
|---|---|---|
| 6. | Raising from seed | 28 |
| 7. | Transplanting | 30 |
| 8. | Crop timetables | 32 |
| 9. | Temperatures | 34 |
| | Temperature regimes. Ventilation. Frost protection. Hardening off. | |
| 10. | Watering & feeding | 37 |
| 11. | Controlling growth | 47 |
| | Growth regulators. Control by watering. DIF. | |
| 12. | Crop problems | 49 |
| | Pests. Biological controls. Diseases. Disorders. | |

**PART 3 Other concerns**

| | | |
|---|---|---|
| 13. | Marketing | 54 |
| | Presentation. Quality control. Pricing. Costings. | |
| 14. | Safety | 56 |
| 15. | Further information | 57 |
| | Sources of help and advice | |

| | | |
|---|---|---|
| Useful conversions | | 59 |
| Index | | 60 |

**Introduction**

This book is intended for all those with an interest in growing bedding plants for profit, including those with no previous experience of the crop. It will also suit those wanting to improve techniques they may already be using.

Bedding plants are commonly known by both English and Latin names. Conventional plant nomenclature calls for Latin names to be printed in italics. However with such a mixture of types in common use, all plant names in this book are printed normally.

I am grateful for the help and patience of my wife, the assistance of many growers and members of the seeds and allied trades particularly Alan Miles of Colegrave Seeds for his contribution to the chapter on marketing and Neil Bragg of Bulrush Peat for his help with the chapters on plant nutrition and feeding.

**Andrew Eames**

# PART 1 Production planning

# 1 Basic considerations

What is a bedding plant? Types of marketing. Seeds, seedlings or plugs? Production facilities.

There are almost as many ways of growing bedding plants as there are growers. The techniques described here are what I think are the easiest and most practicable ways for the less experienced grower to achieve success.

To start with some things may seem only slightly relevant to the growing of bedding plants, but many of the different factors interact. For example, the way you decide to sell the plants may be influenced by where you live and work, while the type of market you are growing for will influence your growing system and the facilities required.

### Do your homework

It is a good idea to think about your motives for wanting to grow bedding plants. Is it because you enjoy growing them? Or is it because you want to make money? The latter is more likely to result in success. A combination of both is better still.

Because it is possible to grow a lot of bedding plants even in a very small polytunnel, some bedding plant enterprises start small, even from premises in residential areas. Remember, however, the friendliest neighbours become 'edgy' when you start a business next door. So if you are starting from scratch remember you may need planning permission.

### What is a bedding plant?

Many would define a bedding plant as 'an annual flowering plant' or something like that. However the term also covers a wide range of plants propagated from cuttings as well (Geraniums being an obvious example) and now the term is generally used to describe anything that lasts for just one season outdoors, or for plants specifically suited to hanging baskets, tubs and window boxes.

## Basic considerations

### Finding a market

There is no point in growing anything unless you can sell it so do your market research first. Find out who your customers are likely to be and - as far as you can - what they are going to want.

There are surprising regional differences. Certain types of bedding will be more in demand in one part of the country than another.

Remember too that the small-scale producer may not be able to compete with larger, more mechanised growers in the wholesale market. On the other hand there is often an unsatisfied demand for lines that require skill to grow, are labour-intensive or both.

### Wholesale or retail?

This is really part of 'Finding a market' and will strongly influence both what you grow and how you grow it.

'Wholesale' in this context means selling to 'trade' customers like garden centres, greengrocers and florists. You can find out what this kind of customer wants by asking them. A good customer will agree a 'programme' with you which will help enormously in planning production. However he will expect a bigger discount and will only enter such a commitment after getting to know you and your plants.

'Retail' means selling your own plants direct to the public and this route means you will have to decide what you think the consumers will buy. The advantage, of course, is that you get the full retail value of the sales. You also get all the unsold plants to dispose of. Are your premises suitable for a retail operation? (Bedding plants do not lend themselves to mail order sales, unlike other garden plants.)

'Wholesale' sales can also be made through a wholesaler like those in Covent Garden flower market or secondary wholesalers who act as regional distributors from primary markets or producers. They normally work on a commission basis and will often add charges for things like transport.

### Seed, seedlings or plugs?

Before thinking about what facilities you will need you will have to decide on the means of propagating. Once there was only one way to start into bedding plants; you sowed seed and raised seedlings. However it is now possible to buy trays of seedlings or 'plugs' from specialist propagators. They cost more than seed, of course, but worries like germination percentages and disease losses are minimised if not eliminated. They save time and reduce the investment in propagation facilities.

'Plugs', sometimes referred to as 'modules', are seedlings grown on into young plants in trays of individual 'cells'. They come in a range of sizes; in their larger forms they are about half-grown.

Both seedlings and plugs offer advantages to the small-scale grower, reducing some of the complication and precision required in the growing system. Plugs offer extra advantages; they are quicker to transplant and tend to produce a better-look-

# BASIC CONSIDERATIONS

ing plant and to do so faster.

The unit cost per plant is more than for seed, although for high-priced species like geraniums the difference between small packets of seed and plugs is often not very much. If you are selling retail the improved appearance may be a very real advantage and the additional cost insignificant.

A combination of these methods may be appropriate, although I strongly recommend the use of plugs for many species. Large growers of bedding plants may raise their own, but the large 'plug' producers are in a very competitive market and pricing is very keen; this is making the buying of plugs more attractive to the small grower.

Some bedding plants are grown on from cuttings and cuttings of subjects such as Helichrysum, Nepeta and ivy and 'zonal' Geraniums for hanging baskets are available from specialist producers.

## The premises

Site is of great importance. It must have good access for vehicles (including an adequate roadway), be well-drained and not seriously over-shadowed by trees or buildings.

Mains services are necessary; you will find life very difficult without water and electricity, and a telephone too.

## Glass or polythene?

If you intend to raise all your plants from seed a glasshouse will be a most valuable asset. However if you choose to use plugs bought in from a propagator, it is possible to grow an adequate crop with simpler facilities, that is to say some form of polythene tunnel.

If you decide the buy a new glasshouse there are some important considerations. Perhaps the most important is to have as large a house as possible; glasshouses are never big enough.

Many small glasshouses (and quite a few large ones) have inadequate ventilation. At least 25% of the roof area should be ventilators- and side ventilators are desirable extras.

Check also on the width of the doors - are they wide enough? - and on the ease of maintenance.

If you are going to raise your own seedlings you will need some staging or benching to work on. A raised area in any case provides a better environment for young seedlings. But beware, glasshouse staging can be very expensive.

Polythene tunnels are widely used - and with great success - for bedding plant production, but most usually for growing-on crops rather than for propagation. Some of the best finished crops are produced in tunnels with ventilated sides. In these polythene is fixed to a batten 2 to 3ft from the ground on each side, the area below covered with netting and fitted with a 'roll-down' strip of polythene to cover it at night or in poor weather.

## Basic Considerations

### Heating

Some form of heating will probably be needed whichever way you choose to grow your crop. The degree of sophistication required relates closely to how early in the season you intend to start and the species you want to grow, but at the very least you ought to have some form of frost protection.

The simplest form of heating - because it is so convenient - is electrical; unfortunately it is expensive to run, although 'off-peak' tariffs can help. Electrical heating may be acceptable for frost protection on a small scale, but it is rare in larger-scale, commercial use, except for propagating beds and benches.

Gas heaters can be excellent and natural gas is still one of the cheapest fuels; bottled gas can also be economic. If you use a 'direct-fired' heater (one without an external flue) do not try to use it for a large temperature lift or you may get plant damage from the products of combustion in the flue gases.

---

**Temperature lift**

Temperature lift is the difference between 'target' greenhouse temperature and outside (or 'ambient') temperature.
The formula for calculating heating requirements accurately is complicated and depends on a large number of factors. Here is how to work it out approximately:

- measure the external area of the glasshouse or tunnel in square metres

- multiple by eight

This gives the heat loss in Watts for a difference of 1C.

- multiply again by the maximum temperature difference required (the temperature lift; usually at least 7C)

This will give you an approximate heat requirement expressed in Watts, which should help when choosing a heater. Remember to add a safety margin, which should be increased substantially for very small glasshouses or tunnels.
You may find heater sizes quoted in Btu/hour in which case use the following conversion factors: 1Btu = 0.293Watts; 1,000Watts = 1kW. So, for example, a heater rated at 100,000 Btu is approximately 30kW.

## Basic Considerations

Other forms of heating include oil, coal and paraffin.

Plants in unheated houses or which have been put outside to 'harden', can be given some protection when frost threatens by covering with a suitable material. Polythene sheeting is not very good for this as it gives little protection against 'radiation frosts', the type which are most damaging in spring. The best and most convenient are spun polypropylene fleece; these are very light and trap a layer of air which affords some frost protection.

Other things you will require are fairly obvious, but do not overlook them. Watering equipment varies in complexity, but the chances are you will still depend heavily on the hosepipe.

Hardware like wheelbarrows and hand tools will have to be kept somewhere and a tool store may also serve as a 'potting shed'.

If you are going to supply other sales outlets you must think about deliveries; this means a vehicle of some sort. However consider hiring; some growers hire a suitable vehicle just for a few weeks and this can be a sensible proposition.

# 2 Boxes, packs or pots?

Deciding what container to finish bedding plants off in is crucial. This container is what the product will be sold in so is part of the presentation and all important sales operation. Traditionally bedding plants were grown and sold in simple wooden boxes or trays. Over the years a greater degree of sophistication has crept in, first with 'strips' (typically five to a standard seed tray size) which created divisions, each holding three to 10 plants). Now, however, there is a strong trend to grow plants with their roots separated in 'cells' of some sort.

This is achieved in a variety of ways, mostly in the form of 'packs' which are designed to double as the sales package. Most of these have been based on a standard British seed tray (roughly 14 x 8in) or a 'half tray', but increasingly there is a range of packs designed to fit in 'outers' which in turn are designed to fit the ubiquitous 'Danish' trolley.

Along with the trend to growing plants in individual containers, there has also been a tendency to lower 'counts', that is to say offering fewer plants in each retail pack; this produces a much better quality product and makes it easier to justify using more costly plant material, including better varieties and plugs.

Increasingly too bedding plants are being grown and sold in individual pots; this is particularly the case with some species, like Pansies.

Boxes and packs are usually made either of expanded polystyrene or high-impact polystyrene (vacuum-formed for thin inserts or trays). Wood is seldom used these days.

Plastics in general but expanded polystyrene in particular has had a bad press in recent years, chiefly because they are difficult to dispose of. However much of the plastics used in plant trays today is re-cycled which is something to tell your customers.

## BOXES, PACKS OR POTS?

Which material is best for bedding plant production is a matter of opinion. Expanded polystyrene is very bulky to store and can be a fire risk, but the boxes are easy to handle and fill. Some growers use their bulk deliveries of boxes, which generally come in neat pallet-wrapped loads, as makeshift additional benching early in the season; of course the benching gradually disappears as the season goes on!

As always, consider what your customers want in the matter of container. Do they want or would they prefer:

- 36, 40 or 50 plants in the one tray?

- five to 10 plants in a 'strip' (four or five strips per tray)?

- expanded polystyrene or vacuum-formed plastics cell trays, with 6, 8, 12, 16, 32 or 40 cells per pack (the modules often split into halves or into individual units)?

- pot-grown plants - in pot sizes from 9 to 14cm diameter?

# 3 What to grow

The bedding plant year - spring, summer, autumn.
Standard bedding plants, Ageratum to Zinnia.

While there are no clear cut divisions we tend to regard certain plants as suitable for one or more of four separate sales periods: early spring (February to March), late spring (April to mid-June), summer (mid-June to late August) and autumn (September to October).

### Early and late spring bedding

There is a useful demand in early spring for plants in flower. This is accounted for almost entirely by Pansies, mostly from sowings made the previous autumn.

A little later in the spring many plants are destined for patio pots and tubs and for hanging baskets. These are examples of high-value products that the small grower can often do particularly well. The term 'hanging basket' covers a wide range; the plastic hanging pots are really only large pots whereas wire baskets are much more complicated and can be works of art.

Tubs are often simply ground-based versions of baskets but can give the opportunity of introducing a wider range of plants, including species which are perhaps not strictly 'bedding'.

Remember that the plants in baskets and tubs have to survive in them for some months. Their compost must therefore have sufficient structure to last this long, and there must be adequate nutrition. Controlled-release fertilisers are definitely recommended - the so-called six-month formulations are best. Water-absorbent polymers are often recommended and do aid re-wetting after drying out, but some of the claims made for them are, in my opinion, exaggerated.

Most bedding plants are used in baskets and tubs from time to time but some are particularly suitable. They include: (raised from seed) Lobelia, Geranium,

## WHAT TO GROW

Impatiens, Petunia, Begonia, Coleus, Gazania, Verbena, Nolana, Thunbergia, and (raised from cuttings) Geranium, ivy Geranium, Fuchsia, Helichrysum, Verbena, Plectranthus, Nepeta, Lotus bertolotti, Scaevola, Lysimachia

This is far from being a complete list and very many other plants are suitable.

For tubs, much larger plants are possible and subjects like Lantana and large Fuchsias and Geraniums are excellent. Small shrubs like Camellias and Bay can also be incorporated.

Finally in the late spring comes the main bedding season when consumers buy their plants for the garden. There is a tremendous peak of demand, lasting only a few weeks, varying from season to season depending on the weather. *This is the time when the vast majority of bedding is sold.*

### Summer bedding

When the spring sales season is over there is a pause. This may be the time to clear up and take it easy, but there is a modest market for some bedding throughout the summer. It is a market which must be investigated before production; some garden centres will maintain sales through the summer, others will not.

The demand in summer is for 'instant' bedding, usually pot grown and often in a large pots, tubs or other containers. The likely customer is one who has come back from holiday, bought a new house, is having a barbecue or party and wants an immediate effect.

Summer bedding must therefore be colourful; hybrid Marigolds, Impatiens, Petunias and Geraniums are particularly suitable as well as plants from cuttings like Fuchsias.

### Autumn bedding

The autumn season has become increasingly important for bedding plant growers in the last 10 years largely thanks to the success of 'winter-flowering' Pansies. These are still the backbone of autumn sales but customers want other lines too.

Traditionally these have included Bellis (daisies), Myosostis, Sweet Williams and Wallflowers. In the past many of these, particularly Wallflowers, were field-grown and pulled or lifted for sale. It is now quite usual to grow them in packs and although some customers will say that these are not as good as field-grown, they are more convenient and popular with garden centres.

Growers and customers are always on the look-out for something different and ornamental brassicas, for example, are subjects that look likely to increase.

### POPULAR CHOICES

Which species and which varieties you grow ultimately depends on your customers' requirements and is another aspect of the bsuiness's inter-relationship.

Generally speaking all the major seed firms and young plant suppliers sell excellent products and apparently competing varieties are often similar. Their catalogues are instructive and often contain a lot of cultural information.

## WHAT TO GROW

I do not intend to try to list a selection of 'best' varieties (my best advice is to attend as many variety trials as you can, whenever you get the chance). However here is a list of the more popular species, with some brief comments.

**Ageratum** These are valued for their blue flowers but there are also excellent white varieties.

**Alyssum** This is the traditional white edging plant, although the range of coloured varieties has been vastly improved over the 'wishy-washy' colours of a few years ago.

**Antirrhinum** One of the oldest of bedding plants but still widely grown. Many types, from very tall (for cut flowers) to dwarf, compact types. Has the advantage that it can be grown (and sold) relatively early which helps to spread out the season. Not easy as prone to root diseases. Often sold in separate colours.

**Aster** Another very large family with a wide range of types. Now less popular than they used to be because of their short flowering period.

**Begonia** This is a large family but we are particularly interested in two main types. *Begonia semperflorens* has many small flowers and is one of the most successful bedding plants in recent years. Flowers are pink, red or white; leaves are light or dark. There are many different varieties with a range of plant height and flower size. Difficult to raise from seed and bought-in seedlings or plugs are recommended. *Tuberous begonias* have large, spectacular flowers, and are often used as pot plants. Difficult to raise from seed and plugs are recommended.

**Cineraria maritima** A relative of the glasshouse pot plant. Grown for its silver leaves.

**Coleus** A species with brilliantly coloured leaves; particularly useful in baskets and patio containers. Some seed strains and 'specials' from cuttings.

**Dahlia** The bedding types have more and smaller flowers than most of the 'garden varieties'. A large subject often used to 'fill in' round the garden.

**Dianthus** A large family which includes garden pinks propagated from cuttings and sweet williams (most of which are treated as biennials and sown in one year for flower the next season). More specifically relevant as bedding plants are a range of seed-raised annual types which are of very mixed parentage. They are showy and perfumed but need a sunny position in the garden to thrive.

## WHAT TO GROW

**Fuchsia** Probably the most popular 'pot bedding' plant. Can be grown from seed but takes a long time to flower, so nearly always propagated from cuttings. A huge range of varieties for many purposes, including bedding, hanging baskets and tubs. Although relatively easy to propagate most are bought in from specialist suppliers.

**Gazania** A spreading, sun-loving plant, very useful in baskets and patio containers. From seed and cuttings.

**Geranium** Strictly all geraniums used as bedding plants are Pelargoniums. For practical purposes there are two main sub-divisions in commercial production, the *zonal* and *ivy-leaved* types. Geraniums have retained their popularity because of their range of form and colour and their early-flowering characteristics. Easy to propagate from cuttings, but because of problems of maintaining healthy stock are more usually bought in from specialist suppliers. Relatively slow to flower from seed and often grown from bought in plugs. Zonals are still probably the most important bedding plant for most people and are widely grown both from seed and cuttings. Ivy-leaved Geraniums are mostly produced from cuttings by specialist propagators although there are some seed-raised types; probably the most widely used and successful basket plant, being tough and reliable.

**Impatiens** ('Busy Lizzie') Improved varieties have made this one of the top bedding plants in recent years. Attractive when on sale and performs well in the garden, especially with some shade. New Guinea Impatiens are more usually regarded as a spectacular pot plant but are proving to be useful bedding plants especially for tubs and baskets; mostly raised from cuttings but there are also seed strains.

**Lobelia** In sheer numbers this is still the most widely grown bedding plant, because of its use for edging, hanging baskets, etc. Valued for its good blue colours but the mixed colours have become more popular. The white, although attractive, always has a few blue 'throwbacks' in it. Trailing lobelia is widely used for hanging baskets, window boxes, etc. but in many cases ordinary varieties are equally suitable.

**Marigolds** A large family which includes the large-flowered African types, both tall and dwarf, the triploids which are vigorous with many medium-sized flowers, and the French types most of which are dwarf and compact with many small flowers. Single and double flower types are available in a range of bright yellow, orange and bronze shades. The 'old English' Marigold, the hardy annual Calendula, is a different species and is now little grown as a bedding plant.

**Matricaria** A dwarf, hardy member of the Chrysanthemum family. Ball-shaped or daisy-like flowers in yellow and white. Often used for edging on large displays.

## What to grow

**Mesembryanthemum** A low-growing semi-succulent with daisy-like flowers. Needs a sunny position.

**Mimulus** Very pretty, moisture-loving plant. Tends to 'go over' but will come again if trimmed back.

**Nemesia** A pretty subject in a wide range of colours. Sometimes short-lived.

**Nicotiana** Improved varieties have made this subject popular once again; sometimes regarded as a substitute for Petunia. Has some unusual colours.

**Pansy** Grown for spring and autumn sales; the latter have become an extremely important part of the bedding season. They come in plain colours and with a 'blotch' and you may hear arguments about which are violas - in practice they are all the same (but see 'Viola'). The winter-flowering types have smaller flowers, and more of them, than the large-flowered which are often sold as pot plants.

**Petunia** A large family with a range of types and colours from the large-flowered 'grandiflora' to the smaller and more prolific 'multiflora', with sizes in between; also doubles and a strain propagated by cuttings for hanging baskets. A successful garden plant but does best in good weather.

**Salvia** Traditionally grown for their red flowers but there are some interesting varieties in other colours.

**Stocks** Certain members of this family are used for bedding, particularly the so-called 'Ten-week' annuals. The newer dwarf types, with a compact spike of scented flowers, are very attractive but are not likely to last a full season. The older, biennial Brompton and East Lothian stocks are generally used for sowing in one year for flowering the following season.

**Tagetes** Small-flowered member of the Marigold family.

**Verbena** Improved varieties have greatly increased interest. An attractive alternative to run-of-the-mill bedding, but not easy to raise from seed. Also varieties propagated by cuttings in a range of colours for hanging baskets.

**Viola** The name viola is often used for the small-flowered members of the pansy/viola family. These are attractive plants with masses of small flowers.

**Zinnia** Very showy, large yellow or orange flowers on rather a formal upright plant. Newer compact varieties look well in pots or containers.

A 'standard' Impatiens (right) alongside the visually more impressive New Guinea type which, however, may not match its performance in the garden.

A major division in Geraniums is between the trailing ivy leaved types (left) and the zonals (the name derives from the zoned variations in foliage colour). Both have been traditionally raised from cuttings but zonals in particular are now also available from seed.

*Tuberous Begonias in flower in a sales pack (left). Growers and retailers tend to hold strong views on the proper degree of flower needed at point of sale but this triumph of the breeder's art begs to be bought.*

*A very different plant from tuberous Begonia, B. semperflorens (right) makes a tempting buy in these six-pack trays showing enough colour to hint at the flowers to come.*

Plug trays, also known as cell trays and module trays, originated in the US where seedlings raised in them are universally known as plug plants or just plugs. Nearly all are made either in polystyrene or vacuum formed plastics (right). Trays are usually specified by a number - eg 576, 286, 180 - representing the number of cells or plugs each tray contains. The 'count' offered by commercial propagators is less than the number of cells in the tray to allow for missing plants.

Transplanting is simplicity itself with these bought-in Impatiens plug plants (above) which are ready to go straight into their prepared growing-on trays (right).

17

Trays of broadcast-sown seedlings (left); even these are available from specialist propagators but whether bought-in or raised on the nursery they then have to be pricked-out, a task calling for a deft touch and some kind of dibbing and firming in tool (below).

The 'mother' outer tray in this collection (centre) is designed to accommodate a variety of inserts. This gives the grower scope to use the same sales tray system for different types of plant.

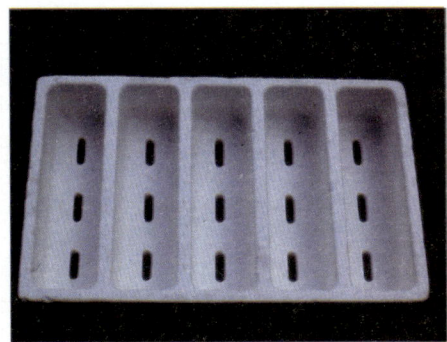

A five-strip polystyrene plant tray (above) and a 40-plant variant (right).

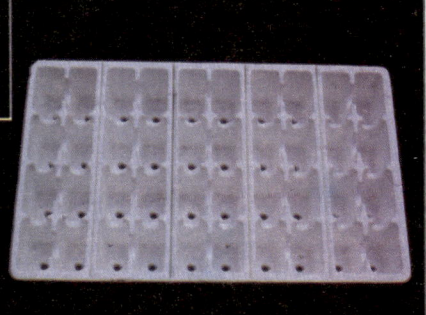

19

Newly planted-on Petunias (above) in a typical polystyrene sales pack commonly known as a 'double-six'; these particular plants will have spent another four weeks or so growing on in the nursery before despatch to the garden centre for sale. The container is a classic sales device inviting the customer to break-off-and-buy at least six plants if not the whole 12!

These Salvias will soon be ready for sale. They illustrate yet another type of sales pack, this one in vacuum-formed plastics which requires an outer tray for despatch and handling.

*This pressed-peat plant tray 'inner' (right) is a biodegradable alternative to plastics and polystyrene.*

Lobelia, Alyssum (above) and, sometimes, Nemesia can be direct-seeded into their final (sale) trays. The advantage is primarily the saving in labour costs through not having to transplant. The disadvantages are that production space is occupied for a long time and the quality of the end product is sometimes not so good.

Two varieties of Verbena (above), a genus which has been transformed as a garden plant by intensive breeding.

Plenty of colour from these Mimulus (left).

### Basket plants
Apart from those referred to separately there are a huge range of other plants suitable for baskets and patio containers. The most important of these include Helichrysum (several varieties), Plectranthus, Nepeta and Scaevola.

### Vegetables
Patio vegetables are sometimes used in a semi-ornamental role. Aubergines, Capsicums, Peppers and Tomatoes can be attractive but the real breakthrough in recent years has been ornamental cabbage.

# 4 The growing medium

Types of compost. Peat philosophy.

Bedding plants are raised and grown on in professional composts (no garden heap material please!). Today the term 'growing medium' is sometimes used to mean 'compost' while in Europe 'substrate' is a common alternative; I shall use the word 'compost'.

### Three basic needs

Bedding plants need three basic things from a compost:

• A sufficiently firm anchorage

• A balance of air (oxygen) and water, so that plant roots can breath and drink

• A balance of nutrients; vigorously-growing plants will need a lot, seeds and cuttings much less

From the grower's point of view a compost should be light, easy and clean to handle, free of pests, diseases and weeds, and not too expensive.

In practice composts fall into two main groups; with loam or without.

Loam-based composts tend to be heavier and are often less well-aerated, but have the advantage of being able to hold greater reserves of water and nutrients. There is also a school of thought that thinks they transplant better, but I believe this is only a very marginal advantage.

Loams used in composts must be sterilised or serious problems will arise from weeds and disease; do not be tempted to try to grow a crop with unsterilised soil;

# THE GROWING MEDIUM

> ## Peat philosophy
>
> Peat has had a bad press. Much of the fuss has been about the loss of our native peat bogs, which are actually only a tiny proportion of the world reserves.
>
> There are sound reasons for arguing that peat should not continue to be used as a soil conditioner for much longer; it is actually not very effective for that purpose and there are a variety of suitable alternatives.
>
> So far, however, there is not in my opinion an entirely satisfactory alternative to peat as a basis for commercial growing composts. Promising alternatives include bark, coconut fibre (coir) and wood fibre. Experimental work is in progress to determine the best ways of using them in composts but it will be some years before we know all the answers.
>
> Having said all that, there is already a limited demand for plants grown in composts without peat. If you intend using them, feeding and watering methods will need to be adapted.

the results will be very disappointing.

Loamless composts are currently based on peat, as it has most of the desirable qualities and is relatively easy to add nutrients to.

# 5 Feeding & fertilisers

Three types of plant nutrition. Proprietary composts.

There are three basic nutrition regimes for bedding plants:

[1]   Base fertiliser plus liquid feeding

[2]   A low rate of a controlled-release fertiliser (eg Osmocote and Ficote) plus liquid feeding

[3]   Controlled-release fertiliser only

Regime [1] gives the grower the best control of plant growth.. Regime [2] is convenient but it will be more difficult to control growth in some circumstances. Regime [3] has the advantage that liquid feeding is unlikely to be necessary but the grower will have even less control.

A suitable formula for base fertiliser for mixing your own compost - regime [1]:

| Ingredients (kg/cu m) | For sowing | For transplanting |
| --- | --- | --- |
| Ammonium nitrate | – | 0.4 |
| Potassium nitrate | 0.4 | 0.75 |
| Single superphosphate | 0.75 | 0.75 |
| Fritted trace element WM 255 | 0.4 | 0.4 |
| Ground magnesian limestone | 2.25 | 2.25 |

# FEEDING & FERTILISERS

These are the amounts (in kg) to be incorporated in one cubic metre of peat. For smaller amounts remember there are 1,000 litres in a cubic metre, and that at the time this Guide was first published, a 'grower' peat bale was about 300 litres (this was likely to be reduced for health and safety reasons; the precise amount should be on the wrapper).

With this formula, liquid feeding will be essential.

For regimes [2] and [3] using controlled-release fertilisers, follow the manufacturer's instructions.

## Proprietary composts

A convenient alternative is to use a proprietary compost in which the nutrient balance is provided by the manufacturer. Although slightly more expensive they take a lot of the hard work out of the job.

Do not be tempted to use a compost with a lot of fertiliser in it in the belief that it will give you a better crop or that it will last longer without feeding. In my experience many problems in bedding plant production arise from using too 'strong' a compost, especially early in the season. Only as the days get longer and the plants grow faster can they tolerate more fertiliser.

Proprietary mixes purchased from the Continent are often lower strength than their UK equivalents, because European growers tend to liquid feed from a very early stage.

If in doubt my advice is to go for a proprietary brand of compost of medium strength for most of your growing. For seed sowing and for rooting cuttings use a 'universal' type with low levels of nutrients.

## PART 2  Growing the crop

# 6 Raising from seed

If you are intent on raising your own seedlings you must ensure that you can get good results; seed is too expensive to waste. So you will need to pay attention to the following ponts.

**Accurate temperature control** is vital and bedding plants need a range of temperatures for optimum germination. For this reason two, or ideally three temperature regimes are needed to cover all the species – 16-18C, 20-22C and 24-26C.

Many seeds are germinated direct in the glasshouse but for a long time **growing rooms** or 'germination cabinets' have been used for the initial stages. These facilities – basically a chamber strongly lit with artificial lights (fluorescent tubes) and temperature controlled – do not need to be very complicated but descriptions of them are outside the range of this book.

The seeds need to be sown in a well-aerated **compost** that contains little fertiliser; even small amounts can inhibit germination. Seed must be sown thinly and seed covering appropriate to the size of the seed.

Some small seeds such as Begonia, are usually left uncovered but this can make them vulnerable to drying. The best **covering material** is a medium grade vermiculite. This is light but holds a humid layer of air in the immediate vicinity of the seed. It also allows light through (some seeds germinate better in light) and reflects sunlight in the glasshouse. This also reduces temperature fluctuations in the com-

## Raising from seed

post. When sowing it is useful to cover newly-sown boxes with paper, plastic or, perhaps best of all, a non-woven fabric.

**Watering** is a problem with newly-sown seeds; they can easily be washed around in the box. One way to get round this is to water the box some time before sowing; otherwise a very fine watering system and great care is required. Larger installations may use 'fog' or 'mist' applications to maintain moisture levels and so reduce the need for watering.

Above all it is essential to achieve good germination or the whole economics of raising your own seedlings become a nonsense.

# 7 Transplanting

Whether you raise your own seedlings or buy in, transplanting or 'pricking-out' is a most important phase in the life of the bedding plant crop. (The term 'pricking-out' is the traditional term for the next stage; it really only applies to seedlings which were, of course, until comparatively recently the only choice; with plug-grown seedlings the term 'transplanting' is more appropriate.)

Seedlings need most care and skill in handling: plugs are not only easier and need less skill but their transplanting is much faster.

When bought-in seedlings or plugs arrive on the nursery unpack them immediately and place them in a shaded glasshouse or tunnel, water well and let them recover and acclimatise to the temperature of your growing conditions.

Pricking-out seedlings or transplanting plugs are operations which lend themselves to simple work study principles. They can often be done much quicker and with less effort by careful organisation. This does not need to be very sophisticated; 'applied common sense' is all that is usually needed. Here are some fairly obvious tips:

•Get your boxes filled and to hand

• Find a comfortable position at the right height (or you will get backache)

• Place both the subject to be transplanted and the box into which they are going close together so that arm and hand movements are minimised.

Whether the job should be done in the glasshouse or at a central point really depends on the layout and nature of the nursery.

# TRANSPLANTING

## Counts per box

How many plants to put in each box has no simple answer; as a general rule plants like Lobelia, Alyssum and Nemesia are transplanted at greater densities than Begonia and Impatiens for example. Many others in between can be in a range of counts, depending on the type of container and the market for which they are destined.

Generally the 'better' varieties (especially F1 hybrids) are grown at lower counts and there is a continuing trend to reduce the number of plants per box or pack.

### Suggested type of container

| | Pots | Packs | Strips |
|---|---|---|---|
| Ageratum | - | • | • |
| Alyssum | - | - | • |
| Antirrhinum | - | • | • |
| Aster | - | • | • |
| Basket plants | • | • | - |
| Begonia semp. | • | • | - |
| Begonia tuberous | • | • | - |
| Cinenaria mar. | • | • | - |
| Coleus | • | • | - |
| Dahlia | • | • | - |
| Dianthus | - | • | - |
| Fuchsia | • | - | - |
| Gazania | • | • | - |
| Geranium | • | • | - |
| Geranium (ivy) | • | - | - |
| Impatiens | • | • | • |
| Lobelia | - | • | • |
| Marigold | • | • | • |
| Matricaria | - | • | - |
| Mesembryanthemum | - | • | • |
| Mimulus | - | • | - |
| Nemesia | - | • | • |
| Nicotiana | - | • | - |
| Pansy/Viola | • | • | • |
| Petunia | • | • | • |
| Salvia | - | • | • |
| Stocks | • | • | • |
| Verbena | • | • | - |
| Zinnia | | • | • |

# 8 Crop timetables

The table opposite needs care in use. It has been compiled in such a way that you can calculate crop timing by working back from the time plants are required for the market. But remember nothing in plant production is absolute and weather conditions, disease outbreaks, equipment failure and the like can all conspire to disrupt the best-laid programmes. May is the peak selling period in many parts of Britain, but sales starts earlier in the extreme South and go on rather later in the North.

Other factors which determine selling time include the customers' planting requirements (eg, local authorities often plant later), the hardiness of the plants involved, even the date of Easter. The opposite table, therefore, should only be used as a rough guide.

There are several other important points to consider:

- sales of hardier species can start sooner

- box or strip bedding needs a shorter growing period than pot or pack bedding because the plants are smaller at sale time

- growing environments can obviously have dramatic effects on rates of growth; they generally grow faster in higher temperatures, but with perhaps loss of quality

- plants grow faster anyway as the season progresses and light gets better

- with plants from cuttings time to sale varies enormously

# CROP TIMETABLES

## Weeks to sale for seed-raised subjects

|  | *Seed* | *Seedlings* | *Small plugs* | *Large plugs* |
|---|---|---|---|---|
| Ageratum | 10-12 | 9 | 7 | 4-5 |
| Alyssum | 6-9 | 4-6 | 3-4 | - |
| Antirrhinum | 11-13 | 7-9 | 5-7 | - |
| Aster | 6-8 | 4-6 | -- | - |
| Begonia semp. | 12-16 | 7-9 | 6-7 | 4 |
| Begonia tub. | 18-20 | 11-12 | - | 6 |
| Cineraria mar. | 16-18 | 10-12 | 7-9 | 5-6 |
| Coleus | 10-12 | 5-6 | - | - |
| Dahlia | 11-13 | 8-9 | 7 | 4-5 |
| Dianthus | 18-20 | 10-12 | - | 6-8 |
| Gazania | 18-20 | 14 | - | 8 |
| Geranium | 14-20 | 12-14 | 9-11 | 5-8 |
| Impatiens | 10-12 | 7-9 | 6-7 | 2-5 |
| Lobelia | 10-12 | 8-9 | 5-7 | - |
| Marigold | 10-12 | 7-9 | - | - |
| Matricaria | 10-12 | 7-9 | - | - |
| Mesembryanth | 10-12 | 7-9 | - | - |
| Mimulus | 10-12 | 7-9 | - | - |
| Nemesia | 12-14 | 9-11 | 6-8 | - |
| Nicotiana | 10-12 | 8-9 | 6-7 | 5-6 |
| Pansy/Viola | 10-12 | 9-11 | 7-9 | - |
| Petunia | 11-13 | 8-9 | 6-7 | 3-5 |
| Salvia | 11-13 | 9-10 | 7-8 | 4-6 |
| Stocks | 6-9 | 4-7 | - | - |
| Verbena | 14-16 | 10-12 | - | 5-7 |
| Zinnia | 5-8 | - | - | - |

Gaps in the table indicate the product is usually unavailable commercially

# 9 Temperatures

Temperature regimes.　　Ventilation.　　Frost protection. Hardening off.

With the large number of bedding plant species, it is obvious that no one environment can best suit them all. Optimum temperatures are sometimes quoted for each species, but as it is rarely practicable to provide ideal conditions for all the plants all the time, some compromises have to be made. The most usual need is for two different temperature regimes.

One regime is in the 15-20C range for tender subjects such as Begonia, Geranium and Impatiens; although these can be grown cooler they will not perform as well and losses will be greater (as well as taking longer to reach selling stage). Otherwise a temperature range of 10-15C is suitable for many subjects.

There are really no hard and fast rules about temperatures; many crops are grown 'slow and cool' with little more than frost protection, and this is particularly suitable for hardier subjects such as Alyssum. But they can be grown fast at higher temperatures too, which can be useful when it is apparent that there is going to be a shortage.

As spring progresses and the temperatures naturally rise, problems may be reversed - plants can grow too fast.

As a very rough guide, **Warm** in the table opposite indicates temperatures in the region of 17-20C, **Medium** 12-15C, **Cool** 7-10C.

## Ventilation

If day temperatures are rising too high, growth will be 'stretched' and plants may spoil and become unsaleable. So it is important to have sufficient ventilation in your glasshouse or tunnel and remember to apply it.

# TEMPERATURES

## Frost protection

As your glasshouse and tunnel space gets used up you will naturally look to see what can be put outside. Hardy subjects like Pansies are no great problem (but try to choose mild days to put them out). Other plants will continue to need some protection if frost threatens.

### Suggested growing temperatures

|  | Warm [17-20C] | Medium [12-15C] | Cool [7-10C] * |
|---|---|---|---|
| Ageratum | • | • | - |
| Alyssum | - | • | • |
| Antirrhinum | - | • | • |
| Aster | - | • | - |
| Basket plants | - | • | - |
| Begonia semp. | • | - | - |
| Begonia tub. | • | - | - |
| Cinenaria mar. | - | • | - |
| Coleus | - | • | - |
| Dahlia | - | • | - |
| Dianthus | - | - | • |
| Fuchsia | - | • | • |
| Gazania | - | • | - |
| Geranium | • | • | - |
| Geranium (ivy) | - | • | - |
| Impatiens | • | • | - |
| Lobelia | - | • | - |
| Marigold | - | • | - |
| Matricaria | - | • | • |
| Mesembryanth. | - | • | • |
| Mimulus | - | - | • |
| Nemesia | - | • | • |
| Nicotiana | - | • | - |
| Pansy/Viola | - | • | • |
| Petunia | - | • | - |
| Salvia | • | • | - |
| Stocks | - | - | • |
| Verbena | - | • | - |
| Zinnia | - | • | - |

* Very approximate guides. Plants listed under '*Warm*' can move to an intermediate environment when established

35

## TEMPERATURES

In a structure such as a polythene tunnel this can be provided by a simple heater; a large temperature lift should not be necessary. Remember that polythene itself gives very little protection against radiation frosts (which will occur with clear skies after bright days); indeed lower temperatures may be recorded under polythene than outdoors.

### Hardening-off

This term is used to describe the transition of plants from a protected environment to outdoors. The need for hardening-off is sometimes exaggerated but it is necessary that plants are robust enough to stand up, literally, on their own and not be devastated by the first gust of wind when put outside. For most plants a few days in a cooler environment before going out is likely to be sufficient for the purpose and generally beneficial.

Traditionally plants have been 'hardened off' in frames which can be covered at nights, but most growers these days have neither the facilities nor the labour to do this.

Covering with anything which will trap a layer of air will give a modest degree of insulation and the polypropylene crop covers or 'fleeces' are frequently used for this. The small degree of protection they offer is often all that is needed.

Water sprinkling is sometimes advocated, but is rarely likely to be effective.

If you are unfortunate enough to suffer frost damage, do not be too quick to throw the plants away; some, such as Lobelia, may make quite a good and rapid recovery, especially if trimmed.

# 10 Watering & feeding

The hosepipe is still the main means of watering bedding plants. Even when other methods are in use it still needs to be available, and for small-scale production is the only method.

There are a number of points to remember about the use of hosepipes:
- choose a good quality hosepipe, one that will not kink or buckle
- make sure taps are in sensible positions
- put posts or rollers on corners, around which hoses will be dragged
- have a suitable 'rose' or watering lance on the end so you do not blast the crop out of the pots or boxes
- if using a hosepipe direct off the mains, the Water Authority in most areas will require you to have a non-return valve fitted so that there can be no possibility of polluted water being drawn back into the system

The amount of water to use is difficult to specify; many growers will just try to water plants as soon as they are dry. This is not always the right thing to do. If plants are growing slowly, for example in cold weather, they may be left dry for a period. Also with some species it may be possible to grow better plants by restricting water somewhat. Petunias are an example.

Over-watering will tend to give lush growth but can also wash nutrients out of the compost. Try to achieve a happy medium.

## Feeding

Unless you are using controlled-release fertiliser, some feeding will be at least desirable and probably very necessary. The only practicable way to do this is to 'liquid feed', and the easiest way is to use a dilutor. With a dilutor concentrated feed is

## WATERING & FEEDING

fed directly and proportionately into the water as it is applied to plants. All dilutors need care in use and in calibration, especially the small ones. Larger dilutors and injectors are generally more accurate and convenient.

Many successful proprietary liquid feeds are available. Make sure you follow the label use instructions; too little is ineffective and too much can easily be lethal.

For most species a feed of 100mg nitrogen, 50mg phosphorus and 100mg potassium per litre can be used once the plants are established.

Later in the season, when the plants are growing rapidly, the feed strength can be increased to 200mg nitrogen, 100mg phosphorus, 200mg potassium.

To mix to the above formula you would need to make a concentrated solution by dissolving 3.4kg of ammonium nitrate and1.7kg of mono-ammonium phospate and 4.6kg of potassium nitrate in water, making it up to 100 litres. This then needs to be diluted at 1 in 200 to provide approximately 100mg of nitrogen, 50mg phosphorus and 100mg potassium to the plants. (The simplest way to increase the strength of the feed later in the crop life is to double the amount of fertiliser.)

*Showing just how large flower heads of New Guinea Impatiens can be.*

*One of the showiest bedding plants emerged when seed-raised Dahlias became available a few years ago (left).*

*Gazania (right).*

*Dwarf forms and new colours have made Nicotiana (left) increasingly popular in recent years.*

*Chalk and cheese - African (right) and French Marigolds (below).*

*Damping off, the classic disorder of bedding seedlings on Pansy (above) and Lobelia (right).*

*Alternaria on Zinnia.*

*Symptoms of rust on Antirrhinum.*

'Silvering' is a genetic weakness of Nicotiana (right).

Uneven development is a typical symptom of pythium evident here in a tray of Antirrhinum.

Petunias (above) mean bold colour and plenty of it.

Surfinia (left), a recently introduced, vegetatively propagated trailing form of Petunia which is ideal for hanging baskets but also makes a surprisingly good ground cover subject.

*Stocks (right), another traditional garden plant which has benefited from the attention of the plant breeders to produce dwarf stocky plants in a wider range of colours.*

*Bedding plants are undemanding in terms of production facilities. Polytunnels like this (below) provide cheap and effective protection which can be conveniently heated.*

Pansies are possibly THE bedding plant if only because, by successional planting they are, in theory at least, available for flowering year-round.

# 11 Controlling growth

Growth regulators.   Control by watering.   DIF.

Having decided how best to make plants grow, it is often necessary to consider how best to restrain growth as well. All too often bedding plants get tall and lanky and can quickly become unsaleable.

## Growth regulators

Three different chemical growth regulators are widely used. They are: paclobutrazol, daminozide and chlormequat. There are several different formulations and they are used in different ways.

Paclobutrazol is sold as Bonzi by Zeneca. It is a powerful growth regulator, dwarfing plants very effectively even in small doses. It is recommended for use on a small range of bedding plants (not all by any means) and must be used exactly as prescribed by the manufacturers or permanently dwarfed plants may result.

Chlormequat is sold as New 5C Cycocel by BASF and as Fargro Chlormequat. It has been used for many years, especially on seed Geraniums (BASF only recommend it for Geraniums; Fargro make suggestions for its use also on some other species). It not only shortens the plants but tends to encourage branching and advances flowering. It may cause temporary leaf marking, especially at high rates. Modern practice is to use it 'little and often'.

Daminozide is sold as B-Nine by Fargro and as Dazide by Fine Agrochemicals Ltd. It is safe to plants and rarely causes damage. It shortens and darkens plants, and in some cases may slightly delay flowering.

With all three chemicals it is vital that instructions are followed. They are all safe to people and animals if used correctly.

You may not want to use chemical growth regulators, and you do not need to. If

## CONTROLLING GROWTH

you buy in plugs, especially Geraniums, they will probably have been treated (ask your supplier what treatment has been applied and when).

Without chemical growth regulators some plants will grow taller than the buyers want these days and may not look so tidy. However it is still possible, with skill, to grow an acceptable crop using crop management techniques to control growth.

### Control by watering

Growth can be contained by limiting water to the plants. This is not often done in the UK (not deliberately at least!) but is common practice on the Continent. If used it must be carried out throughout the life of the crop; it is not satisfactory to suddenly stop watering because the plants are becoming too leggy as the check to growth is liable to be damaging.

### DIF

Plant growth is also regulated by temperature. At its simplest this may mean moving the crop outside to try to slow growth down. If plants are not moved outside there are dangers in trying to use a cool growing environment! It has been demonstrated that plant growth is 'stretched' when nights are cool and days are warm.

Although the mechanism is not fully understood and research on it is continuing, growers have been trying to exploit the technique by keeping night temperatures as high or higher than the day-time temperatures. In most cases this results in plants growing as fast but remaining more compact, although there are big variations and differences between species. This technique is often referred to as 'DIF'; when day temperatures are cooler than night temperatures there is a negative 'DIF'.

This may sound too complicated for the small grower but is very relevant. If your plants are stretching in hot weather it may not help to keep them cool at night. It is the day temperature that matters and the first two hours after dawn have been shown to be the most critical. It may then be very worthwhile to rise early and open the ventilators.

# 12 Crop problems

Pests, diseases, disorders.   Biological controls.

Bedding plants are a short-term crop and are generally not on the nursery long enough to suffer from serious disorders.  What risks there are from pests and diseases can be countered substantially by basic good hygiene. In particular remember to:
* Keep the glass/greenhouse clean and weedfree

* Use clean compost and boxes

* Wash down working areas and bench tops between crops

* Use mains water or water from a source known to be clean

* Do not use seedlings from a box where disease has occurred

* Do not over-crowd or over-water

* Examine any new plants brought on to the nursery (for symptoms of P&D)
With care many problems never arise.

## PESTS
Aphids (greenfly) are the most common pests on the crop. Although found on many subjects at one time or another they are more of a problem on certain species. For example aphids are not easily seen on Pansies and often the first sign of trouble will be crippled and crumpled leaves.

49

## CROP PROBLEMS

High volume sprays of many insecticides are effective, especially if the problem has not been allowed to get out of hand.

Caterpillars are not usually a problem except on Geraniums where they occasionally cause damage when the crop is nearing sale. Hand removal can be effective on a small scale but if there are a large number a high volume spray of an appropriate insecticide may be necessary.

Spider mites are difficult to see and populations can sometimes build up to damaging levels if the late spring is very warm. They develop rapidly in hot, dry weather. Difficult to control with insecticides, repeated treatments may be necessary.

Western Flower Thrips (WFT) is a recent problem which has come from abroad and caused many difficulties to glasshouse growers. It is very small, breeds very rapidly, has a complex life-cycle and is not easy to kill. Frequent sprays of insecticides are likely to be needed. WFT is more of a problem on some species than others; it finds Verbena very attractive.

Most nurseries get WFT by bringing in infested plants; ideally you should have a quarantine area, but short of this careful attention to newly bought-in plants and a spray treatment, if in doubt, may save future problems.

The host range of WFT is extremely wide, and the thrips also transmit tomato spotted wilt virus (TSWV) which can be devastating to a wide range of crops.

### Biological control

Biological control, the use of organisms instead of pesticides to control pests, is generally used on long-term crops like tomatoes but has had some success on bedding plants. Integrated Pest Management (IPM) is the combination of biological control with minimal use of insecticides.

Both techniques need great care, careful observation and regular monitoring if they are to be successful.

Whiteflies are mostly a problem on longer-term crops, Fuchsia being a notorious host. It is important not to let numbers build up.

Sciarid flies are small and black (they are often known as 'manure flies') and can be seen flying around close to the ground. They are very fond of damp places; their grubs live on decaying organic matter, but they occasionally damage plants. Clean conditions and good hygiene will normally keep numbers down.

## DISEASES
Diseases can be grouped according to their method of spread: seed-borne, soil-borne or air-borne.

### Seed-borne diseases
Different species of the fungus Alternaria cause problems on seed of Cineraria Maritima, Lobelia, Dianthus, Wallflower and Zinnia.

Septoria can occasionally cause trouble with Antirrhinum and more often with Phlox drummondii.

Seed companies have adopted treatments to deal with both these diseases and they are less troublesome generally as a result.

### Soil-borne diseases
These cause by far the most losses in bedding plants. Clean boxes and pots, clean well-structured compost and clean glasshouses, benches and handling surfaces will greatly reduce the chance of infection.

Pythium and sometimes Phytophthora cause typical 'damping-off' symptoms; Antirrhinums, Asters and Lobelia are particularly susceptible. The diseases also cause poor and unthrifty growth where root infection takes place after transplanting or pricking out.

Control treatments include the incorporation of a fungicide into the compost or drenches of fungicide after sowing, and after transplanting if necessary. Drench treatments are often recommended for small growers as they are easy to apply and can be used as a routine treatment for Antirrhinums.

Rhizoctonia causes very similar symptoms but often a reddish-brown area can be seen at the base of the stem, and sometimes, with careful examination, a fine web of the fungus can be seen on the surface of the compost. Alyssum, Stock and Wallflower are particularly susceptible. Control treatments include incorporation of a fungicide into the compost or fungicide drench if the problem appears.

Black root rot, caused by the fungus Thielaviopsis, has been more conspicuous in recent years. Infected plants are unthrifty with yellow leaves, and are stunted. On examination, the fine roots will be seen to be distinctively black. It is worse on plants that have been under stress and is a particular problem on autumn Pansies in hot weather.

There is as yet no satisfactory 'cure' but good hygiene and a compost without too much fertiliser will help. Fungicide treatments may help and nurseries with a recurring problem should consider a routine treatment.

### Remember:
- All fungicides are much less effective once diseases have become established.
- Accurate identification of a disease is important as no one fungicide will control all diseases.

## CROP PROBLEMS

• Do not use seedlings from a box with a patch of 'damping-off': disease is present a long time before symptoms appear and it is best to discard such a box.

### Air-borne diseases

Some diseases are spread by airborne spores; microscopic 'seeds' of fungi. These, when they land on a susceptible plant and conditions are favourable to their growth, will 'germinate' and infect the plant.

Good hygiene, starting with healthy seeds or plants, timely removal of diseased material from the vicinity of the crop and an environment favourable to good crop growth, will reduce risks of disease establishment. Sprays of suitable fungicides can help to control disease but it is important to correctly identify the disease and use an appropriate fungicide.

Grey mould (botrytis) affects all bedding plants if conditions are favourable to the fungus; these are cool humid environments with wet leaf surfaces where fungal spores can germinate. The disease tends to establish on damaged tissue.

A range of fungicides can be used, but the disease has become resistant to some, following repeated use, and the use of a single fungicide may be ineffective against the disease.

Mildews are of two types, powdery and downy. They are usually 'host-specific': that is, each only infects one or two closely related species of plants. Identification is not always easy, but their names give you a clue.

Powdery mildews are generally like a fine powder, affecting both upper and lower surfaces of leaves. Alyssum, Cineraria maritima and Pansy are the most commonly affected. The disease is encouraged by warm, humid conditions and often seems worse when the plants are under stress (eg. when watering is erratic).

Several fungicides can give good control if applied promptly and repeated when necessary, but none achieve much if the disease gets out of hand.

Downy mildews are felt-like growths on the underside of leaves: yellowing on the upper surface usually accompanies infection and indicates disease. Alyssum, Cineraria maritima, Stock, Wallflower and Pansy are the most commonly affected. Downy mildews prosper when humidity is high and there is condensation. They are often a problem in poorly-ventilated polythene tunnels and when cool nights follow warm days. Improved ventilation or moving plants outside can result in rapid improvement. There are several suitable fungicides.

Several bedding plant species are susceptible to both types of mildew. Certain fungicides are much better in controlling one type or the other so correct identification is essential.

Rusts, like mildews, are 'host-specific'. They appear as orange-brown pustules on the underside of leaves in warm, humid conditions, often when the plants are crowded. Antirrhinum, Dianthus, Sweet William and some varieties of Fuchsia are particularly susceptible. High volume sprays of fungicides specifically for rusts, help to give control.

Ramularia causes brown or black spots on the leaves of Pansies and Primroses;

# CROP PROBLEMS

usually it is only troublesome in wet, humid conditions. High volume sprays of an appropriate fungicide will give some control.

> **Physiological & environmental problems**
> Not all 'symptoms' are caused by a pest, a disease or incorrect nutrition. Plants sometimes develop 'faults' which may be inherited or induced by the conditions in which they are grown. Where this occurs the term 'physiological disorder' is applied, but it can be used as an excuse for not really knowing the cause. Sometimes problems have an environmental cause: commonly fumes from oil-fired or gas heaters will cause damage.

## Summary of disease control

- Identify disease correctly

- If necessary apply an appropriate fungicide

- If the problem recurs you may have to consider a routine treatment

- Look at and inspect your plants frequently

- Do not get neurotic about diseases!

# PART 3 Other concerns

# 13 Marketing

Presentation, quality control. Pricing and costing.

At the beginning of the book the importance of finding a market and growing only what customers want was stressed. It is vital to identify the type of customer you are growing for, the type of box and/or pot needed, the number of plants/box, whether the plants should be in packs or strips, etc. before you grow the crop.

Having done all this it is most important that your product is well presented. It goes without saying that plants will be in perfect condition and free from blemish; also the boxes are clean, and ideally, every unit of sale (pack, strip or pot) properly labelled. For most customers, labels are a 'must'. Even though they may seem expensive, good labels do sell plants; customers like good, large labels with pictures and plenty of information.

While it is vital to grow what customers want, there are sometimes opportunities to go 'up-market' by offering pot and pack bedding rather than strips. With this kind of business, the margins are usually better. The spring bedding season is very short and specialist growers need to find ways of extending the season. There is a steady summer trade in 'instant' bedding, in pot sizes up to 2 litres, but it is very necessary to have an outlet before growing it. Autumn bedding has also become much more important, but again this is a very competitive area.

Look at the possibilities of 'added value' products, such as hanging baskets, troughs, tubs and other containers. There is usually a good demand for quality products planted up for instant sales appeal. You might also consider contracts for hotels, offices and other local businesses, for supply and perhaps care of planted containers.

Consideration needs to be given to colour. There has been considerable interest

# MARKETING

in colour theming and the use of pastels. Now the swing is to 'designer' mixes of a limited range of colours but with a theme, for example blues or pink/rose shades.

Whatever you do your product must get to customers in good condition. If you are retailing this is rarely a problem, but if you are delivering to a retailer there are two more problems to overcome.

The first is delivery without damaging the plants. If you deliver them yourself this will be your problem but there is always a temptation, when under pressure, to try to squeeze too many on to a load. Large growers are frequently using 'Danish trolleys' which makes handling easier, quicker and helps to avoid damage.

The second problem involves the ability of the retailer to look after your plants. This may be limited and their staff may not know about plants. It is likely to be well worthwhile to take time to teach them that your plants need regular care and watering.

## Costing and pricing

It is straightforward to work out the direct costs of growing bedding plants - it is relatively easy to add up the cost of pots or a box, the compost, the seed or seedlings, the cost of chemicals, labels, etc. It is a little more difficult to work out the cost of labour, heating, water, etc for each pot or box, but it can and should be done. It is the overheads which are usually grossly under-estimated. Not only the office costs such as telephones but also costs of running a vehicle, interest payments on loans, depreciation, and so on can be forgotten.

When you have done your best to allocate all the direct costs, you should probably add on about 50% to cover these overheads and to calculate a total cost. (Don't forget, have you paid yourself for being boss, manager and salesman as well as for your physical work?)

Having done a costings exercise you are in a better position to think about pricing. Unfortunately prices are often fixed on the basis of what other growers in the area are charging. Not all growers do their costings properly and their prices could be unrealistic. Do not be led into the trap of under-charging. Generally there is a good demand for quality bedding and if a customer perceives your product as being what they want, the price is less crucial, especially at the 'up-market' end of the business.

## Remember:

- Do your costings fully and realistically

- Charge everything properly

- Do not be afraid to charge properly; your products and service are better than others!

# 14 Safety

The COSHH regulations affect you. As proprietor you always have the responsibility to behave in business in a sensible way so as not to endanger yourself or others, especially in the use of agrochemicals.

This rule has been formalised by the introduction of the COSHH Regulations (Control of Substances Hazardous to Health). These require employers (and the self-employed) to adopt a systematic approach to storage and use of hazardous substances which means not only pesticides but also any substance which might be a hazard like oils, solvents, disinfectants and even naturally occuring substances such as plant sap.

The Regulations require you to make a detailed assessment of your work activities and identify any areas of risk, then to take appropriate measures to avoid or minimise these risks.

### Remember:
- You must recognise what substances may present risks
- Find out what precautions are needed for each and what are appropriate safety measures
- Ensure that these measures are used and that procedures are followed
- Be up to date with your training and instruct any staff on risks, precautions and procedures
- Keep records of what you have done, including training, risk assessments, information sought and action taken
- Keep a record of periodical safety checks
- For further advice consult your local Health & Safety Executive

# 15 Further information

## Sources of help and advice

If you are going to specialise in bedding plants, consider joining the **British Bedding & Pot Plant Association** (BBPA, 22 Long Acre, London WC2E 9LY, Tel: 071 235 5077)

The BBPA is a specialist branch of the NFU and its membership includes large and small growers. It is a very friendly organisation. It offers a useful Technical Notebook and publishes a regular newsletter which contains technical information. It also has local branches which hold meetings throughout the country.

The **Agricultural Development & Advisory Service** (ADAS) these days is an executive agency of the Ministry of Agriculture. It has a countrywide service, employs a wide range of specialists and can give advice on all aspects of your business. (Find them in your phone book under 'ADAS' or ring 0865 842742.)

The **Ornamentals Advice Centre** (OAC) runs a telephone information service for subscribers, and have a panel of specialist consultants. They are also involved in training courses for bedding plant growers covering such aspects as seed sowing, pricking out and transplanting, growing media, work study, pest and disease control, etc. The telephone number is 0789 472064.

You will also find that suppliers of seeds, plants and sundries can give you useful information about their products; seed and plant catalogues, for instance, can be a mine of information.

Trade papers can also keep you in touch with the latest ideas and technology as

## Further Information

well as giving some marketing information. The **Grower** is published weekly by Nexus Business Communications Ltd, Warwick House, Azalea Drive, Swanley, Kent BR8 8HY (Tel: 0322 660070; Fax: 0322 667633).

Trade shows are also worth attending to see and meet a wide range of trade suppliers. For bedding plant grower the most important are the **British Growers Look Ahead** (BGLA) held at the NEC Birmingham early in the year, and the **Four Oaks Show** held at Lower Withington in Cheshire each September.

Seed companies and plant raisers also hold 'open days' to which growers are invited to inspect new varieties; these can be very useful in keeping up with the latest ideas.

# Useful conversions

1,000 litres = 1 cubic metre

1 oz = 28 grams (g)

1 gallon = 4.5 litres

1 cubic yard = 0.765 cubic metres

1 lb/cu yd = 0.59 kg/cu m

1 oz/gallon = 6.2 g/litre

1 kg/cu m = 1 g/litre

# Index

*italics = illustrations*

**ADAS** 57
Ageratum 12, 31, 33, 35
alternaria *42*, 51
Alyssum 12, *21*, 31, 33, 35
Antirrhinum 12, 31, 33, 35, *42*, *43*
Aster 12, 31, 33, 35
autumn bedding 11

**B-Nine** 47
basket plants 23, 31, 33, 35
BBPA 57
Begonia 12, *16*, 28, 31, 33, 35
biological control 50
black root rot 51
Bonzi 47
botrytis 52
boxes 8, 31

**caterpillars** 50
chlormequat 47
Cineraria maritima 12, 31, 33, 35
Coleus 12, 31, 33, 35
colour theming 55
composts 24, 27, 28

controlled-release fertilisers 26
COSHH regulations 56
costing 55
crop timetables 32
cuttings 5
Cycocel 47

**Dahlia** 12, 31, 33, 35, *40*
daminozide 47
damping off *42*, 51
Dazide 47
Dianthus 12, 31, 33, 35
DIF 48
direct sowing 21
diseases *42*, 52
downy mildew 52

**feeding/fertilisers** 26, 37
Fuchsia 13, 31, 33, 35
fungicides 51

**Gazania** 13, 31, 33, 35, *40*
Geranium 13, *15*, 31, 33, 35
glasshouses 5

# INDEX

grey mould 52
growing medium 24
growing rooms 28
growth control/regulators 47

**hardening-off** 36
heating/heaters 6

**Impatiens** 13, *15*, *17*, 31, 33, 35, *39*
irrigation 29, 37

**loam-based compost** 24
Lobelia 13, *21*, 31, 33, 35, *42*

**Marigold** 13, 31, 33, 35, *41*
marketing 4, 54
Matricaria 13, 31, 33, 35
Mesembryanthemum 14, 31, 33, 35
mildew 52
Mimulus 14, *22*, 31, 33, 35
mites 50

**Nemesia** 14, 21, 31, 33, 35
Nicotiana 14, 31, 33, 35, *40*, *43*
Nutrition 24, 26

**OAC** 57
ornamental vegetables 23

**packs** 8, *20*, 31
paclobutrazol 47
Pansy/Viola 14, 31, 33, 35, *42*, *46*
pests 4
Petunia 14, *20*, 31, 33, 35, *44*
phsiological disorders 53
phytophthora 51
plant choice 11
plugs/plug plants 4, *17*
polytunnels 5, *45*
pots 8, 31
powdery mildew 52
premises 5
pricing 55

pricking out *18*, 30
pythium 43, 51

**ramularia** 52
retail 4
rhizoctonia 51
rust *42*

**safety** 56
Sales periods 10
Salvia 14, *20*, 31, 33, 35
sciarid flies 50
seed 4
seed-raised plants *18*, 28
seedlings 4, *18*, 28
septoria 51
silvering *43*
sowing direct *21*
sowings *18*
spider mites 50
spring bedding 10
Stocks 14, 31, 33, 35, *45*
strips 31
summer bedding 11
Surfinia *44*

**Tagetes** 14
temperatures 6, 28, 34
thielaviopsis 51
transplanting *17*, 30
trays 8, 17, 19, 21

**ventilation** 5, 34, 52
Verbena 14, *22*, 31, 33, 35
Violas 14

**watering** 29, 37
western flower thrips (WFT) 50
whiteflies 50
wholesale 4

**Zinnia** 14, 31, 33, 35, *42*